Falling Down

A Teenager's True Story of Redemption

Daniel P. Kelly

Printed in the United States of America

First Printing, 2013

ISBN-13: 978-1491286371
ISBN-10: 1491286377

Ordering information at fallingdownbook.com

Special thanks to…

Everyone who has supported me in life, my family and friends without whom I am truly nobody.

My parents: we have been through a lot and I hope you understand why I wrote this.

My sisters: I am sorry for what you went through, but I am glad I didn't lose you permanently. I love you both very much.

My grandmother: you fought for me at a time in my life when I needed it most. Thank you. I am sorry you will never get to read this.

My wife: I have had some rough times dealing with my past, but you stuck it out with me and for that I am grateful.

This book is dedicated to all the people who help children in trouble. You have a mostly thankless job, but I want you to know you DO make a difference.

Table of Contents

*There are so many people out there who will tell you that you can't. What you've got to do is turn around and say, **"Watch me."***

- Anonymous

Why I Am Writing This

It is strange writing this. Here I am, 33 years old and sitting here trying to recall the memories I spent so much time and effort burying. I do not want this to come off as a whining account of how my life was hard, nor do I want it to become a rant against the systems in place for troubled families.

This book is a true and uncensored account of my childhood. It contains some graphic stories of what I went through. I hope it helps you understand what happened to me.

What I do want is to give an account of the life and experiences I had as a kid and give some insight about the thinking of a child in these situations. Many books have been written by psychologists and researchers on the subject, but very few are by those who went through it.

I guess I use this as a therapeutic way of dealing with the feelings I have about my difficult experience.

Charles Dickens wrote, "It was the best of times; it was the worst of times." This is how I truly feel about what I went through. I only hope that someone reading this can use it to look at a tough situation and come out of it knowing things will be okay.

Where Am I?

My life sucks!

I'm sitting here in this sparsely decorated room, staring at my roommate, Dave, my Goth, Marilyn Manson-listening, freak roommate. I'm watching him tattoo an outline of his veins while snorting crushed Lithium through a disassembled pen. His hair is dyed black, and he wears nothing but black clothes and combat boots. He told me he used to wear white makeup with black accents, but he can't wear it in this place. Freak!

I must say he is better than my last roommate, Mike, a 12-year-old redheaded arsonist. He set a five-alarm fire in an old warehouse. I remember seeing it on the news. He doesn't even look like he will hit puberty for four or five more years. He claims to have shot someone as well, but in this place you can't believe anyone. They're always trying to talk themselves up around here. Most of it's bullshit.

I'm 16 years old, going on 30; I know everything. I can talk my way out of any mess. I scored in the top fifth percentile on all my standardized tests. I'm smart, private school educated, athletic, religious, and from a fairly well off family. How in the hell did I end up in this place?

Sounds like jail, doesn't it? Maybe the psychiatric ward of a hospital? It's not. I now reside in what the state calls a "residential treatment facility." It's a place to send those adolescents who are not crazy or criminal (except for the arsonist) because there is nowhere else for us to go.

I just got my learner's permit. I can't do anything with it. It's not like they give us access to a car in here. I am the second oldest resident here. I was 15 when the court decided that I was to spend at least the next year of my life here. I was literally weeks away from being too old to be sent to a place like this. Once I turned 16, I would have been outside the court's jurisdiction, and since I was not actually a criminal, I could not have been sentenced to jail.

But, my current fate was sealed two weeks before my 16th birthday. I arrived the day after. Here I was, having just turned 16 and not being able to celebrate it. No candles, no cake, no presents. Most people look forward to their 16th birthday. I missed out.

Only a few more precious weeks, and I would have been free. Instead, I'm watching my whack-job roommate getting high.

My new home sits in a rural town on about 20 acres of hilly property covered in grass. An old mansion houses the administrative offices, the nurse's office, and the cafeteria. The main buildings are old and dimly lit. Narrow hallways seem to snake aimlessly through them. The metaphor of being lost in this labyrinth echoes the reality that I am lost in life. Three buildings serve as residence halls, two male and one female. The gymnasium building has a swimming pool, basketball court, and a weight room. The school that services all the residents of the campus is a series of four trailers on the edge of the property.

I use the word "campus" lightly. The word denotes that it is a beautiful place where everyone is free to do as they please and no one has a care in the world. It is a nice place, but it is far from carefree.

I have a job here that's not bad. It's cutting grass and odds and ends maintenance work. I'm all-important because at 16, I get to use the riding mower. They pay us below minimum wage, and we have no choice but to do the work. It feels like prison, but at least I have something to do.

I guess it's better than jail, which is where I was headed. A Division for Youth facility was likely going to be my home for the next year or two. Someone, somewhere decided I was worth saving, so I ended up here. Ironic, as I never committed a crime still I was going to end up in "kiddie jail."

They say no good deed goes unpunished. That is why I get the freak and the arsonist for roommates. I am one of the "good kids," so instead of getting my own room I get to be a good influence on these idiots.

Awesome.

The Beginning

I wasn't always headed down this path.

At the age of nine, I moved into a nice home in an expanding suburb of western New York State. All the houses looked the same with manicured lawns, new cars, and lots of kids. My family was typical, consisting of two younger sisters and my typical middle-class parents who were married and living together. It was nothing special, and nothing strange.

I, on the other hand, was a nerd, just a geeky kid with big ugly glasses. My parents wouldn't let me get cool ones because I tended to break them. I didn't do anything different from most kids my age. I rode my bike a lot and roamed the neighborhood, where I knew no one. In fact, I rode into the woods and got lost twice in the first week we lived there, and I was brought home once by a pizza delivery guy. My parents didn't seem to care.

When school started, my third since kindergarten, I met my first friend, Adam. He lived one street over, and I was instantly accepted into his group of friends. My parents didn't like him though, claiming he was a bad influence.

So there I was, a relatively average, though slightly nerdy, kid in suburbia. What could possibly go wrong?

From a very young age I was a free-spirited, independent kid. I needed to have a set schedule from the moment I woke up or I would do what I wanted, when I wanted. Once I got control of my own time, I was nearly impossible to bring back into a structured setting. I was not a huge discipline problem, but I liked attention. I was once sent to the principal's office for tying my own shoelaces together and pretending to trip. I did it to get a laugh, but that was the extent of my misbehavior in class. I have also been told that I did not turn in my homework in school. It wasn't for a lack of doing it, as my parents would always check. Even so, I would tell the teacher that I didn't do it. I suppose this was for attention too, although I don't remember doing it at all.

I know you're reading this saying, "This is a typical kid, what is the big deal?"

Nothing. Until typical is no longer the norm.

Hit Me. I Dare You

I acted up at home. A lot. Nothing big, just a lot of little things. The problem was not how I acted, but how my father handled it. I was spanked often as a kid. It seemed that this was the only way he knew how to discipline me.

When I did something wrong, I knew what was coming. But I started to get paranoid when I was at home. I didn't always know I had done something wrong, so I did not always know a spanking was coming. This made me constantly think about whether I was going to get it at any time, and I started to withdraw and avoid my father much of the time. I thought if I avoided contact that I could avoid punishment. This was not successful and in many ways made things worse. I began to feel that it didn't matter how I acted, I would be in trouble anyway.

I remember one incident very clearly. It was Christmas Eve. It had snowed a little over a foot that day, and my father went out to shovel the driveway. My father had told me to do it, but I argued about having to go out and shovel. In part because I was a kid and in part because it was Christmas, I didn't want to do it. It wasn't an abnormal reaction. However, it pissed my father off something fierce. He made me go up and clean my sisters' room, even though I had my own room and they weren't doing anything but playing downstairs. I was not happy about this so I grabbed one of my books, stomped into my sisters' room, laid down between the bed and the wall, and began to read. About 40 minutes later, my father stormed I yelling, "Why haven't you cleaned their room?!" I thought that was the end of it. I went into to my room to get ready for church. He came a few minutes later holding his thick leather belt. I had never gotten the belt before. I was scared to death. I normal spanking was bad enough; I knew this was going to be a painful experience. Needless to say, I was not at all comfortable sitting in those wooden pews in church that night.

The belt became my father's standard method of discipline. This continued for the next year or so. I began to resent him, and as I was starting puberty, and the punishments were humiliating as well as painful. To make matters worse, he would talk about it with his friends from church while I was in the room. I continued to withdraw. My refuge was in the basement, usually with a book or an old television we kept down there. I would do anything to try to avoid punishment. This included screaming, running, and holding on to anything I could while he was pulling my feet. This only delayed the inevitable and probably made the punishment worse.

Things were getting out of control with my mother now too. One morning before school we got in an argument about something minor (I don't recall what), but it escalated into a fight that ended with her lying on top of me choking me with both her hands. My head was pressed up against a chair and I told her she was going to break my neck. Her words still ring in my ears. She said, "Good! I hope you die!"

I'd had enough. When I got to school, I asked how I could report abuse. The counselor asked me what had happened and I told her about the incident with my mother and what was going on with my father. The counselor saw the marks on my neck and some marks on my lower back and buttocks from my recent run-in with the belt and immediately called Child Protective Services (CPS).

CPS conducted an investigation into my claims. I was not privy to the interview with my parents, so I don't know what was said. What I do know was that my parents sat me down and told me that if I did not ask that the case be dropped, I would not be allowed to see any of my friends and all my extracurricular activities would be gone. The next meeting with CPS was with my parents and me. I was asked if I wanted to continue with the case, with my parents sitting in the room staring at me. I was only 11 years old and powerless to see my friends if they said I couldn't. I said no and the case was dropped.

Life in my house went well for a while, but eventually returned to the status quo. The arguing and hitting began to escalate. I was angry and began to rebel more now. I was apparently too old for spanking and my father began to slap me in the face. This turned into being backhanded. It became so frequent that I started to have problems with my jaw. I was hit anytime I said or did anything that my father didn't like.

I continued to withdraw and would often go into the woods to smoke cigarettes to escape my life. I wanted to leave, but had nowhere to go. I was depressed and wanted life to be over. I fought back. I argued with my parents over anything I could. I refused to do chores or anything I didn't want to around the house. I was tired of feeling like a scapegoat for all my parents' problems. If I got in trouble with my sister, she got grounded, but I got hit. It was time to make a stand.

I was a freshman in a private high school now because if I stayed in public school, I would have failed. I had new friends and had all but forgotten about the old ones. My grades were passing at best, and I acted up a lot. I started smoking cigarettes regularly now and would leave school with some friends at lunch to smoke across the street. I took the anger I had towards my father out on other students at school and was more than once called into the principal's office for bullying, and I began to skip classes and school.

Things at home were increasingly worse. All the while, my father was teaching parenting classes at church. I hated him. I hung out with the rebellious crowd. I loved the freedom I felt when I was with these new friends. Although, I still had to go home. Things there were bad. Constant screaming, fighting, and hitting. Soon I was big enough to challenge my father. I thought if I could fight back he wouldn't hit me. If I pretend to not be afraid I would be safe even though I was truly scared of him. I thought this would somehow help me survive the nightmare I was living. It didn't.

The hitting became wrestling, shoving, and throwing and breaking things. I once had a chair thrown at me so hard that all four legs stuck in the wall. I, of course, had to patch up the holes in the wall. I wasn't sure how much more I could take. I began to antagonize my father to get him to hit me. I wanted a chance to hit him back and show him what it was like.

That chance would soon be gone.

Death Sounds like a Plan

It was a normal sunny, August day at my house. I still remember it as if it was yesterday.

I was told to mow the lawn. I had taken to arguing about everything. This time I was angry that I had to do all this work around the house to get an allowance while my sisters didn't. It escalated into our usual screaming and swearing. Then my father hit me for the last time.

We were in the garage fighting. He smacked me in the face with his hand, and I picked up the nearest object I could find, which happened to be a metal baseball bat. I told him that if he touched me again, I would kill him. He continued to come at me, and I started swinging to keep him back. He threatened to call the police so I ran into the house and disconnected the phone in the basement.

I snapped. The only way I could think of to not hurt anymore was to die. I truly didn't know how else to feel ok. I felt trapped in a house where I felt unsafe. I didn't think that I mattered to anyone, especially my parents. I would not be missed and my family would be happier with me dead.

My father started to come down the stairs so I grabbed my pellet gun and fired a shot to keep him back. I then started to look for his shotgun. I didn't want to hurt anyone, just end my own miserable suffering.

I found the gun and the shells. But there was a problem – the barrel had been removed. (My father later told me that he took it off and hid it because he thought I might do something. I always wondered why, if he was worried I might do something, he didn't get me help.) I frantically tried to find the barrel, but to no avail.

I was contemplating other ways to kill myself when the police arrived.

An officer came down the stairs and talked me into dropping the shotgun I was still holding. He began to talk to me about the consequences to my family if I killed myself. He described what a room looked like when someone used a gun to commit suicide. He told me of the pain and the guilt that the survivors experience. He explained to me that my parents did care if I lived or died even if I couldn't see it.

This reached me, and I broke down. He stayed with me, talking to me about what was going on until I calmed down. He took me upstairs and discussed our options with my parents. I agreed that I needed help and should go to the hospital. I went to the psychiatric unit in the back of the police cruiser.

If I had known I could have fired that shotgun without the barrel on, I would not be here today.

I maintain to this day that the officer who talked to me saved my life. He was kind and talked to me like an adult. I was fortunate enough to meet him about six years later and thanked him for what he did.

I'm Crazy Now

The psych ward is a strange place to be. It isn't what you see in the movies. You know, people drooling and talking to imaginary animals. My institution was all kids. It looked like a hospital, smelled like a hospital, and was dead quiet. It had the sterile feeling of a typical hospital, but with carpet and table lamps. It had the false warmth of a funeral home, except it had locks on the doors and thick metal security screens on the windows. By the time I got through my initial evaluation and was brought upstairs, it was three in the morning.

I went into the lounge of the unit. I had no idea how long I was going to be a resident here, but I knew I needed help, and I was glad to be out of my house.

I was not allowed to have anything that I could use to hurt myself or use to runaway, which included my shoes. The one thing I remember most was the ridiculous slippers they gave us to wear. Bright yellow foam with big smiley faces on them. As if I didn't feel crazy enough.

I woke up in the morning and got to see my new room in the light. Two desks, two closets, two beds and a night stand. It had its own bathroom and shower, which was cool, but when I looked out the window, I saw the metal grate covering it. Through the metal was a view of the city from the fifth floor of the hospital. I guess it was so we didn't jump out. I didn't have that urge now. I felt safe there and was looking forward to getting some help.

My roommate was my age and was pretty cool. We exchanged the usual psych ward introductions of how we ended up there. He gave me the low down on how things operate in the place and which staff members were cool and which weren't.

There was a level system in place that allowed residents to advance depending on time in the institution and behavior. To move up you basically just had to be good and participate in therapy. Some of the kids tried to kill themselves while I was there. A few even made a pact to do it together. One girl electrocuted herself in the middle of the night. She lived, but spent a week in a padded room. She would keep us up at night screaming.

I did as I was asked and tried hard to share my feelings and get to the bottom of why I felt the way I did at home. I wanted to get better. As a result, I quickly moved up to the top level which allowed me to order food from outside the hospital, go outside on visits, and stay up later. Privileges were like gold in an institution like this, and I was happy to have them.

We had daily group counseling sessions and the main topic revolved around drugs. Many of us talked up our experience with them. I learned a lot about drugs there and I was almost starting to believe the things I said to be cool.

After a few days, I finally met my doctor, a man who paid no attention to the pleadings of his patients and assumed there was something wrong with us just because we were there. This idiot set the next five years of my life in motion. I do not use the term idiot lightly here. He went against everything he was trained to do by diagnosing me with Bi-Polar Disorder and Oppositional Defiance Disorder. Did I mention that this guy diagnosed me without ever talking to me? Yes, you read that right. The first time I met him he informed me of my diagnosis within five minutes of introducing himself. I tried to tell him what life in my house was like from my perspective, but he didn't seem interested. He instead just contradicted everything I said with statements my parents had made. He made me feel like a liar, like I was making everything up. I was feeling better in this place and he was making me feel like it was entirely my fault.

The labels he placed on me would not only haunt me for years to come, but it would lay the groundwork for the biggest chip I think it is possible to have on one's shoulder. Later, I discovered I had not been diagnosed correctly, but for now I had to live with this hanging around my neck.

I was a moody, defiant 15-year old. Abnormal, huh?

So there I was, on medication for depression, which I didn't need because I was out of the situation that made me depressed. Ironically, I learned how to abuse these meds to get high while in a psychiatric ward.

The biggest thing I learned how to do there was lie. And lie I did. I learned that the bigger the lie and the more detail that was injected, the greater the likelihood it would be believed. I learned how to manipulate people on an almost sub-conscious level. I did this to make myself look cool around my peers. Call it a giant game of one-ups-manship: one guy did something, so I did better.

As this game progresses you incorporate other people's stories into your own. Tell them enough, and you start to believe it yourself. Believe enough of them, and you have created a new reality and self-identity. I was no longer the weak, attention-starved little kid. I now had more attention than I ever wanted. It was time to unveil the new me.

Free At Last! Kind of...

Three weeks. I was in the hospital for three weeks. I was safe. I finally slept well. I had positive reinforcement for three weeks. Now I was going home. But what had changed?

I was going home. Had home suddenly become a safer and better place to live? I doubted it could be any different in that short amount of time, but was hopeful. Regardless of my feelings, I was going home.

The only good thing about the embarrassment of being in the psych ward is that your parents also share it, so lying about where you have been is easy and your parents cannot dispute it. I told all my friends that I was in rehab for alcohol and marijuana. It was an easy out that made me look cooler around my friends. I was "Dan the Rehab Man."

I came out with more confidence than I had gone in with. I also came out a different person. I was a cool guy who, armed with the experiences and lies of other people, set out to create a shell that would cover my pain and allow me to create my outgoing, carefree, and successful alter ego.

I told lie upon lie, mostly in an effort to ward off the questions of my three-week absence, but I liked the attention the stories brought. I enjoyed my friends thinking I was cool and not looking at me like the crazy friend who just spent nearly a month in yellow smiley-face slippers. I needed the lies. They made me feel better about who I was. This allowed me to appear stable on the outside while the fragile, scared, self-conscious, and often suicidal kid remained on the inside.

My parents also changed. Gone were the people who thought that they had somehow made a mistake and helped me down the spiraling staircase to hell that my life had become. Now they had their cause.

It was genetics. The doctor said I was bi-polar, it had nothing to do with my home environment. Gone was any responsibility for their actions or guilt about how they handled the situation. Now it was about controlling the demon inside me. And they had help.

Many states have a family court-run program for monitoring troubled youth. This is not for serious criminals, but for shoplifters, truants, runaways, and kids whose parents are unable, or unwilling, to control them. In New York, it is known as Persons In Need of Supervision, (P.I.N.S.). All my parents had to do was file a petition with the court, and armed with my most recent suicidal actions and threats about how I would not be able to leave the house if I fought it, the court quickly decided I needed supervision and on probation I went.

Probation. I had never broken any major laws, but I was on probation. I went once a week to see Rick, my probation officer, who actually carried a gun. I was ordered to stay in school and attend drug and alcohol counseling. This action was the beginning of the end for my living with my parents. A stay that was shortened by a well meaning, but idealist therapist.

For the sake of anonymity, let's call our "family" counselor Dr. Frank. He started our attempt to regain some semblance of family cohesion by telling us that "sometimes families just can't stay together." While I agree that this is true, it became a self-fulfilling prophesy to me. We must be one of those families, otherwise why would he give us such an ominous disclaimer.

Our sessions were generally spent blaming each other for the incidents that occurred at home that week. Inevitably, they would digress into screaming matches followed by someone crying and storming out of the room. Every week ended in a stalemate with neither side willing to give in to the smallest of requests. It always felt as though the counselor was just another person in my life telling me that I was the one to blame and my opinion didn't matter. If there was a difference in the account of events, than I must not be telling the truth.

I felt the need to always be defensive, and I truly never felt heard. Here we were in counseling, rehashing events that had already occurred and discussing feelings that had already been hurt. We rarely, if ever, discussed the reasons the arguments happened in the first place or how we could have avoided them. There were no coping strategies to work on during the week, no conflict resolution skills, and no tools to de-escalate tense situations. It was just a war where the battle lines had been drawn and there was no compromise or concession. It was a war of attrition and no one was winning.

Gone was the hitting, but in its place was a practice that would make it impossible for me to stay at home. The new strategy for dealing with conflict at home was not to work through it, but to involve other people. This first meant calling Dr. Frank, who I was not allowed to call or speak to, so he only got my father's version of events. This then shifted to the police being called for everything from an argument to my unwillingness to perform chores. I felt ganged up on, constantly being told that I was the one who had to change and just accept it. I was not willing to just lie down and pretend that I was the only person who was doing anything wrong.

I wanted desperately to be heard. I wanted one person to truly listen to me and not run to my parents to report what I said. I felt utterly alone.

I was in a house with my family, but couldn't tell them how I felt for fear I would end up back in the hospital. If I told my friends, I would disclose what was going on and unravel the stories I had told. My "doctor" would only tell my parents. The constant fighting, screaming, and crying contrasted with the deafening silence about how I felt inside.

The more I felt that I didn't have a voice, the louder I became just trying to get someone to hear me. No one was on my side. I fell deeper into depression and tried like hell to avoid the black hole of despair I had fallen into before I had tried to take my own life. I was losing the fight and I knew it. I had to get out by any means necessary. But I had no idea how and I had no one to guide me. I was quite literally alone and in fear for my life, not from my father or the courts or the police, but from myself. I was self-destructing and I needed and escape.

I found temporary relief in a very strange place.

Rehab

I needed an ally. I couldn't count on my parents, lawyer, counselors, probation officers, pastor, or any other adult in my life. I needed someone who could advocate my needs to my parents on my behalf. I found this in my drug and alcohol counselor, Sue.

Prior to my stay in the hospital I had little exposure to drugs and alcohol, aside from the occasional party where I forced down a beer in order to impress my friends who were doing the same thing to impress me. I had seen marijuana a few times, but had never smoked it because I thought I might get into trouble. I had managed to turn the occasional cigarette into a pack-a-day habit, but that was the extent of my substance abuse. This was not the information I gave to my substance abuse counselor. She heard the version of me that was fabricated through tall tales while I was in the psych ward. While in the hospital, I had met some interesting characters. I watched the strong kids and tried to figure out what it was that made them stand out and earn the respect of their peers. It boiled down to experience and I had none.

I was a good kid, even with all the internal strife in our house; outwardly we were projecting the illusion of a strong family. Things were at a critical mass at home, but the folks at church thought we were as normal as they come. I was active there, an usher on Sundays, helped during vacation bible school and played on the church basketball team. I believed then in what I was being taught and really tried to follow it. As a result, at 15, I could not compete with the stories I heard from my friends in the hospital. I had never had sex or done drugs. My alcohol intake was limited to a few beers. I had to borrow some stories and reinvent myself if I was to convince them that I was indeed abusing drugs.

I gave enough detail to convince Sue that I had a problem with alcohol and I needed to see her on a regular basis and needed to go to group counseling sessions. I finally had a place to speak openly to people who were looking out for only me and not reporting back to my parents. I had to learn to cope and this was going to give me those skills.

One of the few remaining coping mechanisms I had to get me through a day was cigarettes. This was a huge source of contention and arguments in my house. I was building toward two packs a day, and I had to steal them from a local grocery store in order to maintain my supply. My mother called them "cancer sticks," and my father was sick of me throwing them in the lawn. I had a coffee can on the side of the garage for my butts, but my mother threw it out because she didn't like it. I was losing the fight to keep my coping mechanism and one of the only freedoms I had left. The court said I must have negative drug tests and since I had never smoked pot, this would be a simple enough task. My counselor had told me that quitting multiple substances at the same time would lower my chances of success. Smoking is one of the hardest addictions to break and it took me another 15 years to finally do it, but at the time was the only real addiction I faced.

I asked my counselor to help convince my parents that I needed to continue to be allowed to smoke. My parents, emboldened with the knowledge that they could report me to my probation officer for the smallest of infractions, were even less flexible and unwilling to budge on anything that I requested. I had to take a giant risk, openly admitting that I was committing crimes on a near daily basis in an attempt to convince them to allow me to keep one of the things that was keeping me sane. My fear was that this would get back to the court and get me sent to a DFY facility. I had to chance it.

I convinced my parents that I had a significant problem with drugs and alcohol and genuinely wanted to quit. My counselor informed them of the facts surrounding quitting multiple substances and my parents very reluctantly agreed to allow me to continue smoking, but because of their moral objections, refused to buy them. I am still amazed by the fact that my parents morally objected to buying a minor cigarettes, but his stealing them with their knowledge (and often in their presence) was okay.

I had won a small, but important victory. I had proven to myself that I could effectively manipulate people to get the things I needed. I also learned that my parents were still going to do what they felt they had to in order to maintain their absolute control. I had to find a way out. I had a small ally in Sue, and I could use my continued "sobriety" to lend some credence to my efforts to reform my behavior, but I was still in a toxic environment and needed a way to get someplace safe. That would take a while.

I'm Not Crazy! Am I?

Things at home were tense to say the least. There was an uncomfortable stand-off, but relative calm and no one wanted to upset the proverbial apple cart.

I understand my parents' desire to find something wrong with me and therefore take the blame off anything they may or not have done. We tried investigating food allergies, which only caused me to eat rice cakes for a week and just be really hungry while being angry. My friends were limited to weed out the "bad influences." This was ineffective because my friends weren't influencing my behavior at home. Now I was on my third psychiatrist in a few months (we changed whenever my parents felt that the doctor wasn't doing what they wanted), and I was really starting to resent the implication that I was broken and everyone else had no responsibility in what was happening at home. At the same time, I was beginning to feel that I was the sole cause of everyone's misery and there was nothing I could do about it because I had some sort of chemical imbalance.

I still had no advocate other than my substance abuse counselor, who had used all her clout to keep me in cigarettes. The purpose of the psychiatrist was to regulate my ever-growing and changing list of medications that were supposed to fix my behavior and make me "normal."

The trouble with psychiatrists is that their job is primarily to make sure that the medications are at therapeutic levels and that they working to correct the issue. Many people hold out hope that a little pill will alleviate the symptoms they presume are caused by a disorder. When the pills don't work, they either have to accept that the disorder isn't there or the doctor is doing something wrong. My mother led the charge here. In her view, the medications had no measurable effect, so it had to be an issue with the doctor.

I was now seeing a new shrink and I did not like her at all. She was very dismissive of any opinion I had and was only interested in medicating me into submission. I was on pills to stabilize my mood and for depression. These are some intense drugs that are designed to alter the brain chemistry. This came into play one night when some strange things happened.

I had never done any illegal drugs, but I had taken a few pills when I was in the hospital. The most I got out of it was a buzz, and I stared at a red blinking light on top of a radio tower for a while. Nothing had ever prepared me for what I was about to experience.

I was outside having a cigarette before bed. I remember it being a typical early winter night: clear, crisp, a few scattered clouds lit up by a very bright full moon with a halo around it. What happened next I still can't explain. Maybe I took too many pills by accident, or maybe the drugs were starting to mess with my head.

I was looking at the clouds and I watched them change color. At first it was a just to red, and I thought that my eyes were playing tricks on me. I thought it was the brightness of the moon, but then they changed color again. I wasn't scared until they changed to multiple colors. It was no longer just the clouds but everything around me. Everything on the street seemed to glow, and I lost perspective on distance. I must have been out there a long time because my father came out to check on me. It was obvious that something was wrong, and I was so scared that I told him what I was seeing. I saw the northern lights later in life and while similar to what I saw that night, he couldn't see it. Something was wrong. I was crying, and he hugged me and told me it would be okay. I thought for a moment it would be. I had told my father what I was feeling for the first time in a while, and I thought that things would work out all right.

The next morning, I was hospitalized again.

This place was different. It was older than the last hospital. It was dimly lit and filled with the shadows of a staff that remained distant. I hadn't done anything to warrant being there. I get that I had hallucinated the night before and that my parents were pretty concerned about this new symptom of my "illness," but I couldn't understand why I to be there for what was being described as a medication adjustment.

I was pissed. I wanted no part in any discussions, no sit down with yet another psychiatrist who was on staff there, no desire to talk to the other kids, and certainly nothing to do with my parents. I was honest about something and it got my back in the looney bin. The only redeeming quality of this place was a small closet with a punching bag in it. I spent hours in there trying to work out the rage and nicotine withdrawal coursing through my veins. I took the pills they gave me and retreated into my own personal hell. They gave me a reason to be angry and a justification to start keeping my intentions from anyone who could stop me. Suicide was back on the table and escape was my priority. Although no one knew it, I was willing to risk everything to get out of my house. I was afraid that the longer I stayed at home, the less I would be able to be honest about my feelings. I desperately needed somebody to talk to, someone I could trust with my true feelings. The longer the despair remained buried, the more dangerous I felt.

I spent my days in group therapy sessions where I acted withdrawn, in individual sessions where I acted belligerent and angry, or in these ridiculous "meditation" sessions where we just slept. They seemed like an excuse to round up all the kids so one adult could watch us while the rest went out and smoked. Even meditating made me angry. All I thought about was the ridiculousness of my situation. The anger turned inward. "If I had only kept my mouth shut…" The only solace I had was the room with the punching bag and I spent hours in there.

After a couple of weeks I decided to play along. It became obvious that in order to get out I had to do what they wanted and act complacent. I buried my emotions deep down and did as I was expected to. I confessed to anything they accused me of: lying, thoughts of harming myself, and my deep-seeded anger. The anger part was easy; I just had to pretend it was at my "condition."

After another week of crying myself to sleep and hiding every emotion I had, they let me out of the hospital because I was no longer showing negative emotions and my medication must have been working.

Reinvention

One of the hardest things to do is convince yourself that what you are doing is the best thing to do even though you don't want to do it. Deep down I loved my parents and knew that they loved me. I wanted their approval and their support and for things to return to normal. The latter was impossible. There was a lot of anger and resentment on both sides and it was all justified.

I had to get a support network that could help me cope with my anger and stop a dangerous spiral. My current friends were unable to help. Their parents were friends with mine from church, and they had no clue what was going on beneath the pretty picture we presented. I had a few friends at school, and I started to hang out with them more. We all smoked and would leave school together to do it. I started to drink in school, usually some nasty liquor poured into empty contact lens bottles. I also tried weed for the first time. I found it ironic that I became a "bad" kid in order to escape the situation at home where my parents thought I was already doing the things I had just now started to do.

I was not allowed to date until I was 16, mainly because my father was hyper-religious. When I was a sophomore in high school, I began to date a girl in secret. I would frequently fight with my parents about the dating rule. I can remember some pretty vicious and violent fights about it. I wanted justification for the rule, but all I ever got was that his friend from church, "has the same rule for his kids. Why can't you just follow it like his kids do?" The rule just didn't make sense, and since I was dying for someone I could confide in, the rule made that harder. We would go out when I was supposedly with my male friends or when I was supposed to be at a school function. I just wanted to feel loved and needed by someone.

I got comfortable enough with my friends to be very honest with them, and I explained my situation. I told a very one-sided version of events that cast my parents as monsters and me as the victim. The pretenses may have been exaggerated, but the result was the first support system I had been able to enjoy in quite some time. They were also mine. My parents didn't know them, so I could have my secrets and no one would report my actions to my parents.

My parents thought that since I met these new friends at my Catholic school that they were good kids, and they were, just not by their standards.

These new allies accepted of me for who I was, and they were from a little tougher walks of life than I was used to in my friends. My confidence was surging, and I was starting to take pride in myself. I was truly an introvert, but around friends I was able to be outgoing. I was discovering a new coping skill: ego.

I was started to develop a second personality as a protective shell. Inwardly and privately, I was a scared kid whose parents tried to control even though I was really trying to be a good person. My shell was protecting the fragility of the introvert inside me. My ego was growing to the point of narcissism. I cared little about those around me who didn't support me the way I needed. I was becoming a fun person and I liked the power I had socially. I felt normal around my friends. I wasn't afraid to speak my mind and was completely unafraid of authority figures.

At home, I had rules, but most were arbitrary, and many were unfair. My father had adopted a tough love philosophy and was sticking to it. I just thought he was a bully. I was only allowed 10 minutes on the phone at a time, although I could call someone back immediately. My sisters did not have this restriction. I had a curfew, but since I needed a ride everywhere this was not an issue. The police were still regular guests at the house and the arguments were becoming more explosive. I had taken to going to school on my terms, sleeping in if I wanted to and going only if I felt like it.

I was exhausted most of the time. My home life was rough and keeping up my persona of the kid who didn't care was taking its toll. I pierced my ear, which got me locked out of the house for a bit. I grew out my thick, curly hair and was now smoking more than two packs a day. I had to smoke outside and preferred the cold to being in the house with my family.

I was getting blamed for everything in my counseling sessions. My depression was becoming a real problem, but I couldn't tell anyone. I was back to thinking that death was a good escape, and I was scared. If I confided in my counselor, I would end up in the hospital again or worse. I had to find a way to release the pain and anger I felt inside, and I was desperately trying to find a way out of my house and into an environment that made sense to me. There seemed to be no options, and I was becoming desperate. But who could I tell?

Not Again

A part of being on "mood stabilizing" medication is blood testing to ensure that the levels are correct. I was taking my pills as prescribed, and I was having blood drawn quite frequently. I did not like the meds nor did I like the continuing feeling that I was broken and needed fixing. I didn't understand how, if I had some mental illness, I was being blamed for the actions that resulted from this illness. You don't blame a cancer patient for getting sick, why was this different?

I was sitting at home on a Friday morning. I had not gone to school that day, and I was sitting in the living room playing a game on the computer. My great-grandmother was in the hospital after suffering a fall at home. We knew she would not leave the hospital alive. I remember my mother coming in and telling me that she had died and I would not be able to go to the funeral because I would be going back into the hospital myself. I was confused, unable to grieve the loss of a relative (or say goodbye), and I was angry. I began to yell and cry, which only served to reinforce my mother's opinion that I needed to go. At this point, it seemed any emotion or anger at all was cause for at least a discussion about how I needed to go to the hospital. My parents were looking for a drastic and immediate change in my behavior. It seemed as long as I acted like a drugged up zombie, my parents were happy. I don't know what their model of a perfect teenage son was, but it certainly wasn't me.

I returned to the same dark, dingy hellhole of psych ward that I had been in last time. They had removed the punching bag so I had no physical way to work off the rage I had within me. To make matters worse, I had been admitted on a Friday so there was no doctor on to talk to me about my grief for the death of my great-grandmother, my anger for being in the hospital again, or the confusion as to why I was here in the first place.

Apparently, my last blood test had shown a level of zero, as if I was not taking my pills, which led to my new stay in an institution. Regardless of what the test said, I had been taking them all along. So I was subjected to the humiliation of proving I was taking them by sticking my tongue out every time I took a pill to prove it. My anger was growing.

The trouble with anger is that it isn't really an emotion. It is a reaction to another emotion. The truth is that I was hurt. I had been hurting for years. I felt abandoned, and now I was dropped off on the assumption that I was intentionally skipping the pills that I was ordered by the court to take. No one would listen to me, and I just wanted one person to believe me.

The hospital's doctor seemed to not understand why I was upset. I was missing the funeral, being falsely accused, and in a hospital for something that could have been handled at home. Even when taking the medicine under supervision at the hospital, my levels did not come up and that fact only made me more vocal about the injustice of my being there. They increased the dosages of my medications and eventually doubled them in order to get the levels up. I was vindicated in that I had proved it wasn't my not taking the pills that caused the problem, but I was still in the hospital. It was clear I needed someone outside to help me now. I needed a lawyer.

Luckily, since I was on probation, I had one. I called her and explained the situation, and she promised to get me out. In the meantime, I threatened to sue everyone who was involved in keeping me in that hospital. I was out in less than two days. The previous psychiatrist who didn't listen to me anyway was gone. I guess my parents figured she wasn't able to "fix" me either so it was time for a new one.

School Sucks

Up to this point, I skated through school. I barely passed when I didn't just outright fail, and I put no effort into course work of any type. It wasn't that I was lazy; I had worked since I was 12. I did odd jobs and lawn work for a local music store, worked for my grandparents' company cleaning up their shop. I was bored out of my mind.

I was tested early in school and my parents were informed that I was in the top five percent in the country. I tell you this not to brag, because it really means nothing if you don't use it, but to help you understand why I was bored. I could pass the tests without studying, keep up on class discussions, and read faster than most. I spent much of my childhood reading anything I could get my hands on.

Falling Down

My parents told me about my academic potential. Well, more accurately, they wouldn't let me forget it. They repeatedly told me I should be doing better in school.

My teachers usually didn't like me. I was disruptive, and I didn't do work. I had the ability, but I wasted it daydreaming about what could be. My home situation didn't help matters. I was tired, stressed out, and I had bigger things on my mind than an upcoming math test.

I had been pulled from public school and sent to the school at my church where the teacher (who was also the principal) was a close friend of my father's. Had I stayed in public school, I would have failed and been forced to repeat seventh grade. The smaller setting was good for me, and the teacher was able to give me work that was challenging. The school only went up to eighth grade, so for high school, I would have had to go back to the district I almost failed.

My friend was going to a Catholic high school and he seemed to be doing well, so I convinced my parents that his school would allow me to be more successful. They agreed, and it started off fine. I was motivated and had discovered sports. I was still bored and was a C student, but was not failing. My freshman year went without much incident. I had received a weeks' worth of detention for skipping school, but nothing worse than that. My home life was deteriorating, but it hadn't yet digressed to the level it would soon become.

It was the summer of my sophomore year when I was first hospitalized that school became less of a priority. I had so much going on at home that I didn't want to be at school either. I didn't want to be anywhere. My 10th grade year started out fairly normal. I played soccer, but my smoking was having an impact on my play. I had to deal with the now frequent absences as a result of being in the hospital. They didn't have actual school in the hospital, so I was falling well behind the other students. I could no longer rely on my retention of class lectures because I was missing too many days. I was now failing everywhere. Home was getting worse and now one of the places that I used to able to escape feelings of inadequacy at home was making me feel like I could do nothing right.

I decided I would rather just not get up in the morning and stay home alone. The house was empty and I had a TV in the basement, so I could retreat down there and escape the things in life that made me depressed. This became my solace, a place I couldn't be touched. I just stayed there, listening to music and smoking cigarettes. I took to drinking during the day and eventually only left the basement to eat and sleep. The time alone didn't help my depression at all.

I spent much of my time in the dark. A fitting analogy for what my life was becoming, a dark place that I could not get out from under. I had missed weeks of school now between two hospitalizations and just not going. I had no doubt that passing my sophomore year was not going to happen. I started looking into other options.

There was one job that I really thought I would be good at. I wanted to become an electrician. I heard of a place called Job Corps where I could earn my GED and get training as an electrician. I could live there and solve many of my problems. I had finally found a way to get out. The one problem was that I needed to convince my parents of this.

My mother would frequently tell me, "You're too smart to be an electrician. Those jobs were for people who couldn't get into college!" I would argue that my father didn't go to college and he was doing just fine.

She would reply, "That's different. You need to go to college."

College! I was about to fail high school. I was so depressed that I wanted to just sleep all day and when I was awake I thought about dying. College was never going to happen. I only wanted to get into another environment where I could do something with my life and be happy.

Many roadblocks had been placed in my way and now my own parents were stopping me from being successful. I was going to die if I stayed here, and they were intentionally keeping me right where no one wanted me to be anyway. Did they *want* me to die? Just blame it on my so-called mental illness? "We tried, but he was just too sick." Jesus!

I was done. I'd had it. I had to be 16 and not in school to go to Job Corps. I had five months until I was old enough. Now I just had to quit school. Easy.

I just came out with it one day. I was no longer going to school. "Don't wake me up, I'm not going." My parents were done too. We were all tired of the fighting, tired of the yelling, tired of the cops coming all the time. Since I went to a private school all they had to do was de-enroll me. Hell, it saved them money. My father even told me he supported my decision, until he reported me to my probation officer. I asked him why he would do that knowing it would cause me to be removed from my home and probably sent to jail. He said, "Of course I still support you, but I didn't say you could still live here." For a moment I thought he would actually support me. Instead, he was playing word games.

I needed to find a place to go that would allow me to get out of the house and avoid the inevitable consequences I was now facing. Fear became terror; despair became desperation. I had not thought this one through. I had forced their hands and finally stepped in it. I had gone too far. I went from being belligerent and toying with the conditions of my probation, to openly violating it.

My friends couldn't help me at this point. I needed to ask someone for help. I needed the biggest favor in history. I needed a miracle.

I went to my grandparents and asked them to let me live with them. I brought my extended family into a situation that they had only been on the outskirts of previously. They knew there were issues, but had not gotten involved. Now it was a full-blown crisis. My grandparents and my aunt and uncle offered to take me, but my parents saw that as giving into me. I was in no position to make demands, and they knew it. Going to stay with family was inarguably the best option, but they were angry and wanted me to pay for the damage I had inflicted over the years. I had to be punished, and if that meant jail, so be it. If that meant writing me off, they had two other kids. I was on my own, and since they could make the decision, I was stuck.

I went to my grandmother and begged. I pleaded with her to let me come and live with her. It was the lowest I had ever been. I needed someone to give me one last chance. My lawyer had failed to keep me off of probation so I had no faith in her ability, but my grandmother could hire her own. I asked her to sue my parents for custody. It was my last chance. She was reluctant. She knew what the inevitable consequences were and that we only stood a 50/50 chance of winning. I had thought of this earlier, but it would have ripped my family apart, and I didn't think she would say yes. It was a last resort.

My family was now suing each other, and I was smack in the middle of it.

Full Circle

It was going to take some time for the court to figure out what to with me. I had dropped out of school, violating a major condition of probation, and now multiple members of my family were willing to take me in. I would have to wait find out my fate.

In the meantime, I definitely could not live at home. My parents would not allow me to stay with any relatives, presumably so I couldn't claim that I was already living there when we went back to court. With nowhere else to go, I ended up in yet another hospital. I knew I didn't need to be there, and this time, I was not angry. I was scared about where I was going to end up, but I was, at least for now, in a safe place.

The anxiety of the unknown wasn't helping my mental state. I was still seriously depressed, but I was not thinking about suicide. I was limited in who I could speak to now. My parents could decide who could visit and call into the psychiatric unit. I was now in regular communication with my lawyer who was working on options and trying to find a place for me in the meantime. I did have a girlfriend at the time. Given what I was going through she, understandably, wanted nothing more to do with me. It didn't help the depression, but I also didn't have time to dwell on it.

I could not stay in the hospital long. There was nothing clinically wrong with me and they needed the beds for kids with more immediate problems. I was set up with Child and Family Services to find me a place to live in the interim while we were in court. This is where I met Michelle who would be instrumental in the coming months. Her job was to make sure I was safe, and she answered directly to the court. She was working on getting me moved to a shelter for runaway children. My parents were vocally against this because they would no longer be able to make decisions about my day-to-day actions. I could speak to whomever I wanted and go where I desired.

I spent three weeks in the hospital without incident. I was now avoiding contact with my parents. I would see them when they came to visit because I had to, but going home was no longer an option. I had no reason to try to make them want me to go there.

This would prove to be my last hospitalization, but I had no idea what I was in for.

Sheltered

Upon leaving the hospital, my new residence was an older house in downtown Niagara Falls. There were three bedrooms upstairs and a living room, dining room, kitchen, and staff office downstairs. I had a small bag with a few pieces of clothing. It was all I owned. I had a room to myself for now. That would change as kids came in and out of the shelter.

The house was in an older section of town. When it had been built it was probably the nicest house on the block with large columns on the front and high ceilings. The front yard was probably once very nice, but was now small because the road had been widened several times and the flower beds were now overgrown and mostly dead.

My room had two sets of bunk beds and a bare light bulb on the ceiling. The walls were covered with old textured wallpaper that had probably been white at some point, but 40 years and numerous residents later, it was now a dingy brown. What little carpeting the house had was either cheap commercial carpet or was threadbare with patches of the backing showing through. The TV was ancient and surrounded by obviously donated furniture. There were two mismatched couches and a couple of chairs. They all had different styles and fabrics and the ones that were not covered with a sheet were stained and torn. The dining room table had eight or so chairs from eight different sets. At least I had furniture. It wasn't much, but it was home.

I was one of three residents when I arrived; there would be as many as eight during my stay. We were all broken. Some of us were in trouble with a court of some kind. A few were being protected from parents who were seriously abusing them both physically and sexually.

I was absolutely forbidden from disclosing the location of the house itself. I was not even allowed to tell people what street it was on. We entered and left through the back door and used the alley to come and go. People picked me up at the grocery store a few blocks away.

I had little or no contact with my parents, not that they seemed to want it. I was in a place where they were not allowed to know my location and were not able to control my actions. For the first time since all of this began, I was free from the control of my parents and free from the restrictions on whom I could see. I finally had people who were working on my behalf. People who were doing things based on my needs and not acting on what my parents said was the "right" way. I was free, but I wasn't in school or working. This had to be fixed or there was no way the judge would let me go anywhere that was not a group home or jail.

My parents had pulled my enrollment in the Catholic school so I was not enrolled in any school and given my situation, I couldn't enroll anywhere. For now, I was stuck at the mercy of decisions I couldn't control. I needed to focus on my own mental state for a while.

Being homeless was a strange thing. I wasn't homeless in the sense that I lived in a box in some alley panhandling for money to buy food. There are different ways to be homeless. I was not allowed to have a home. The unusual thing is that I have no bad memories from this place. As I write this, I remember all the places and situations I was in and they all have good and bad memories associated with them. This place has only positive ones, save one: the food.

It was a small community-based agency that ran this shelter and a couple more in the city. There was not a huge budget, and we relied on donations for the majority of our food. I remember the local donut shop used to donate the donuts at the end of the night instead of throwing them away. They would come in a trash bag, but we didn't care. They were good donuts. But to this day I simply cannot stand the thought of Hamburger Helper®. It's not that it is terrible, but I swear, we ate it every night. I appreciated the food, but I just can't eat it without going back to that time.

I was happy, which was weird for the situation I was in, but I really was. No more arbitrary rules that seemed to just be there for the sake of making rules. I was no longer stealing cigarettes on a daily basis. I was able to buy them. I was able to see friends that I hadn't been allowed to see previously and reach out to family that I wasn't allowed to contact before.

There was one thing that really helped me put things into perspective. One thing that took away all my anxiety and depression and made me want to survive this chaotic period in my life. Niagara Falls.

The honeymoon capital of the world. A place that many people come to celebrate the beginning of their lives together. Unfortunately, many people also come here to end theirs. I had a choice to make. I could walk right to the edge of the falls in about a half hour from the shelter. We needed to check in every six hours, so I had about five hours to take in the beauty of the place. I went there almost every day.

If you have never been to the Falls, you are missing one of the most spectacular places on the planet. A near 200-foot drop into either the water or onto giant boulders that have broken off from above as the water continually erodes and reshapes the precipice. Heavy, impassable rapids above and below serve to magnify the raw power of the water falling into the gorge. Mist is everywhere and the roaring sound of the plummeting water can be deafening. Tourists mill around taking in the sights without a care in the world, never knowing that the Falls have a dark side. People come here to contemplate and commit suicide. That was why I came here.

I was always astounded by the majesty of Niagara Falls, but I had never seen it for more that was it was. It was always beautiful, but nothing more than falling water. Now it was a metaphor for my life. My life was the water cascading over the edge of a cliff.

As I stood at the edge, a calm came over me. I realized how truly insignificant my problems were when compared to the grandeur of what I was standing next to. I could see why people chose to die here. This would be a great sight to make my last.

The height from the observation tower is dizzying and the fence protecting you from a long and fatal fall to the bottom is only 3 or 4 feet high. I stood here for hours wondering what the end would be like. A simple hop over and a few seconds in the air and all the pain would be gone. What would the end feel like? Would it hurt? Would I be afraid as I fell?

A wave of calm flowed over me as I accepted that these would be my last moments. What did I have to live for anyway? My life had become a disaster, my parents had abandoned me, and I was going to go to jail because I didn't go to school, which I now wanted to go back to, but my parents had pulled my enrollment. I would show them. They would blame themselves. They would feel the pain and anguish that I now felt.

I WOULD SHOW THEM!

I would prove that I could make it in spite of their attempts to control my future and in spite of them wanting to be in charge rather than doing what was best for me. I would show them.

I backed away from the edge never to return. I would take what the court decided and prove that I wasn't some delinquent who only had jail in his future. I would survive and live on my terms. Gone was the scared kid; I was confident. I had gone to the edge and decided that I could be more than just another dead kid who had just taken too much. I had to get through the next stage in life, but I was determined.

I would survive.

Court

Family court is an interesting animal, especially when you are not actually charged with anything. The judge has almost unrestricted authority and it often pits families against each other. I was represented by the attorney my grandmother hired in an attempt to gain custody of me. My parents had hired a lawyer to defend their right to decide what happened to me.

This is the hardest part of my story to articulate, and it would define my relationship with my parents for many years. It would also lead to one of the hardest emotional issues I would have to deal with in life. An issue that continues to haunt me today. I had been dropped off in hospitals, lived in a shelter and now was about to go to jail. I had not, until this moment felt truly abandoned. I had the option to go live with my grandmother, but my parents were actively trying to make my life miserable. They would prefer that I go to what was quite literally jail rather than go to a place that was safe and I could try to start over.

I want to be clear. Much of this story is from my perspective as a teenager. But when I say jail, I mean it. This was the place that kids went after they murdered people. They were just waiting until they were 18 and could go to Attica. There were bars on the windows, locked doors, violent kids, and no escape. This was not the place that a kid, who at worst had shoplifted some smokes from the neighborhood supermarket, belonged. I don't know that I would have come out of that place in any position to succeed in life. This is what was at stake.

My parents were willing to send me there in order to win a fight. Instead of listening to the people that said this was not a good option – doctors, lawyers, counselors, my probation officer – they wanted to be in control and would not listen to anyone with whom they disagreed. I had a chance to go to a safe place, but they were deaf to the advice of professionals and the pleas of my family and me. They wanted to win.

They held the cards. I had dropped out of school so I was in a weaker position and it was difficult because everyone acknowledged that a structured environment was needed for me to be successful. It was hard sitting in court and hearing my parents talk about how terrible I was at home. A lot of things had happened over the last year. Most of it was terrible.

I had fought for so long to control my life that I came across as a monster. I tried to bring up the abuse that occurred in the house, but the judge said "We all have skeletons in our closets. My father hit me too." It became obvious that I was going to lose. I had my grandmother's support, and I knew that she would be there for me no matter the outcome.

It was never an option to return home. My parents made that perfectly clear. The judge ruled that he agreed going to my grandmother's would have been a good option, and he would have granted that request because it is always better to place a child with family then to place them with the state... if I had been in school. He recognized that it was now April and there was no way I could complete the year and he wanted more stringent monitoring of my academic progress. My dropping out of school had gotten me away from that house, but it became a case of out of the frying pan and into the fire. I was going to jail and there was nothing I could do to stop it.

My only other hope was for a residential treatment center to take me instead, but that would be the center's choice. I had a pretty colorful past and they generally didn't take kids with both mental illness with violent behavioral outbursts and an apparent lack of regard for any authority.

My parents said things in court that were at best exaggerated and at worst outright lies. They said that I broke curfew all the time even though my mother would complain that I never left the basement and that always scared her. My outbursts had been blown out of proportion and the violence done to me was justified. I had also tried to use a gun to kill myself, and I had significant rage issues. The group home was not going to accept me. Jail it was.

Salvation came from an unlikely source. I didn't particularly care for my probation officer. He was a gruff, no nonsense man who wasn't there to make me feel good. His job was to make sure I followed the rules. I never saw him as an ally, and I didn't know he was one until years later. My grandmother and I were obviously upset about where I was headed, and she went to him to plead for a better option. She was told not to worry about it, that it was taken care of. I never did get the whole story about what happened, but I know that someone was pulling for me. I could only confirm portions of this later, but I had enough information to know that he played a major part in getting me there. Kiddie jail was out and instead I was off to a group home.

My life was about to dramatically change again. The judge had ordered me to spend a year there. This was not a flexible time frame, essentially a sentence. I was anxious, but I had a date to look forward to. It was only a year.

My grandmother still looked at is as jail. I had a sentence, and I couldn't leave. She made this point to my mother and was told that it wasn't jail.

"Well what happens if he leaves?" she asked my mother.

"He gets arrested," was the reply.

"Well that's jail," my grandmother insisted.

This led to one of the funniest moments in my life.

It was my 16th birthday. I had been allowed to get my learner's permit that morning, and I was going back to the shelter for my last night before I moved to the group home. I was driving, and my grandmother and I were talking about staying positive and getting through this year. We both started crying and she said, "Happy birthday – you're going to jail." I had to pull over because we were laughing so hard.

The next morning I would be moving into my new home and a new chapter in my life. At least I knew where I would be sleeping for the next year.

I'm Home

I toyed with the idea of naming this chapter "Crossroads," because that is where I was. I had a choice to make, comply with the rules or buck the system. I had been doing the later for the better part of 16 years. Given my current situation, it wasn't working so well for me. I had to make a conscious effort to follow the rules and do what they wanted me to do. I decided to give in and do what my parents wanted. I just wanted to go home. I wanted an end to all of this and maybe this would give me and my parents the tools to make a successful transition home a year from now.

The group home operated on a level system. At level one, you were restricted to the cottage mentioned earlier. At level two, you could walk around the campus unsupervised.

Reach level three and you could walk to the hot dog joint up the street, get a milkshake, and get off campus for an hour. Level four was the crown jewel: you could leave unsupervised for up to four hours. The mall, fishing – it was up to you how you spent the time. The only catch was you had to work to obtain the higher levels.

My first week was spent hanging around the cottage. Playing pool on an old snooker table, playing cards, watching TV, and meeting my fellow residents. There were eight of us on each side of the cottage, which was divided down the middle by a wall and the staff office.

We had to keep our rooms clean, and they were inspected daily. If you didn't keep it clean you would have to go to bed early, and you wouldn't be able to stay up late on the weekends. I started making my bed for the first time in a long time.

There was a school on campus. The few trailers weren't much to look at, but there were some good teachers. It was the end of April, and I would have to work my butt off to not fail 10th grade. I had until the end of August to do it, but what else did I have to do?

I leveled up as fast as it was possible to do so. I raced through the levels, I kept my room clean, I was respectful to other residents and staff, and I worked hard in school. I was happy and I was safe. I was rewarded for my hard work and actions instead of punished for my shortcomings. I was thriving.

I was doing so well in school that I passed my sophomore year and was allowed to go to public school in town. I still had to live on campus, but I rode a bus and went to school like a normal student. I was determined to prove my parents wrong and be successful. I felt like a success for the first time in a long time, maybe ever.

After six months of living on campus I was allowed to move to a house in town. It was owned and staffed by the group home, but it was a regular house. We cooked our own food, did our own dishes and washed our own clothes. It was almost normal. There were only six of us there and a few of us had part-time jobs in the community. It was the best I had ever had it.

I was never in trouble and I was on the honor roll with perfect attendance.

I often credit the group home with saving my life. I mean that. It was a wonderful place from which I hold no bad memories. The staff and the structure helped me go from the worst point in my life to the best. I was surviving in spite of the issues I had before, I was making something of myself.

The Fight of My Life

The only thing that wasn't successful was my relationship with my parents. We were in counseling, but we still spent the entire sessions rehashing old fights and blaming each other. They still ended in tears with no resolution.

In a strange irony, the same psychiatrist who had originally diagnosed me as bi-polar was on staff at the group home. I had none of the symptoms of the illness there, proving that they were not caused by mental illness, but from the situation and the environment at home. I was flourishing here and I was NOT mentally ill.

The focus in the sessions with my parents continued to be filled with resentments and blame. This translated to my home visits. I was allowed to go home on the weekends and could stay from Friday until Sunday. I don't recall an instance where it went that long. Many visits ended within minutes and resulted in my father turning the car around a few miles up the road and dropping me back off.

The visits were supposed to be a bridge to the ultimate goal of returning home. We were supposed to work out our issues as we would have to when I came home the next year. There was a big problem: it wasn't home anymore.

I have two younger sisters and when I left home; my room was given to my youngest sister. If I did manage to stay overnight at my parents', I had to sleep on the couch. I was a guest. It was their home and I wasn't a part of it any more. There was the promise that *if* I returned home, they would build a room in the basement for me. I realized that returning home was not a forgone conclusion, and I may need another option. I was only to be in the group home for a year. Where would I go after that?

One of the things my parents liked about my current location was their ability to once again decide who I was allowed to speak to and who I wasn't. They stopped me from speaking to certain friends, but most importantly, they stopped me from seeing or even speaking to my grandmother. At the insistence of my counselor, I was allowed to receive and mail letters and packages. Otherwise, they felt, it would be too large a distraction to our goal of me returning home.

We endured months of unsuccessful home visits, including a terrible Christmas break where I was not able to stay for longer than two days. I was even almost brought back on Christmas Day after threatening my father because he slapped my sister.

I was upset that I didn't have a room at my parents' house and yet I was supposed feel welcomed there. I had more rules there than I did at the group home. It was supposed to be practice for my eventual return, but it was still the same old place I had left. Only this time, instead of calling the police, they threatened to take me back. This threat was repeated often. I was supposed to be perfect and happy. It didn't matter how I actually felt. I was supposed to act like I wasn't a guest in my own home. I was supposed to be happy about sleeping on the couch and walking around on eggshells for fear of having to go back to the group home. I was torn between wanting to be happy and wanting to be home. But I was starting to see my room with the freak roommates as home. That became my normal, and I was happy there.

At the group home, I was trusted to spend time unsupervised out in the community. At home, I couldn't even leave the yard. Why would I want to spend my weekends at home with less freedom than at the place I used to consider jail?

I had to look at other options. I was still a kid and I wanted to please my parents and have a relationship with them. I truly wanted to go home, but I could not return to their house if it was going to be more of the same. There was a lot of hurt and resentment on both sides. Unless that was forgiven and we were going to move on, we were doomed to fail. I couldn't afford that. I decided I needed to reopen my option to go to my grandmother's house when my year was up. I just needed a way to do it.

I voiced my concerns to my social worker, who was working to get me home, but had been witness to all the struggles we were having. She agreed that it would be a viable option with the court as long as I continued making the progress I was. The biggest issue was communication. Legally my parents were allowed to block my ability to speak to my grandmother, and mail took too long. I was in the new house in town and there was nowhere near as much supervision. My social worker told me that if I was to "run into" my grandmother at the mall, then there wasn't much anyone could do about it.

So I arranged it. I called her from the house and told her that I could meet her at the mall and have lunch. We met a few days later at a little pizza restaurant. It was the first time we had seen each other since my birthday in April and it was now January. I asked her if she would be willing to go back to court and try again. I was confident that we would win this time as the deciding factor the last time was school and now I was not only in school, but doing well. I was even enrolled in a trade program to become an electrician. On top of that, I would be 17 and have served the one year as ordered and fulfilled all the conditions imposed by the judge.

I brought this option to my parents who opposed it and were adamant that I would not go to live there. I asked them what my other options were if I didn't go home. They said I could stay at the group home, but the group home said I didn't meet the criteria to stay. So my parents said I could go into foster care.

Foster care? I couldn't believe it. My parents would rather me go live with complete strangers than with family. They would rather I go live in one more place than lose to my grandmother. Disbelief was an understatement. I was devastated.

That night I was pretty upset. I was crying heavily and I drew the attention of the night staff member. I explained the situation to him and how I was upset because my parents were against what I felt was the best thing for me. I still wanted their approval. He gave me a hug and told me the words that would get me though the challenge of fighting them in court, "Fuck 'em, do what's best for you." He was right. I needed to do what I needed to do to become successful, and I could no longer worry about my parents' ego.

As the court hearings progressed, it became clear that I was going to be able to go to my grandmother's, and my contact with my parents lessened. Our family sessions seemed to focus more on my mother's relationship with my grandmother and little was mentioned about me coming home. Spring break was a big test. My parents were still fighting my contact with my grandmother, but I was talking to her regularly. I was just not allowed to visit. It was becoming inevitable that I was going to be going to my grandmother's, but we, along with my social worker thought it would be best if I stay there on weekends in order to ease the inevitable transition. My parents were against it, but my social worker was able to convince them that it was the best option. I was able to spend the entire spring break there. Life was finally coming together for me. All the hard work was about to pay off. Just one more hurdle to go...

The judge had to agree.

Life Begins At 17

It was almost my birthday. My year was almost up, and I was sure I was going to be going to my grandmother's. But it was not certain until the judge said so. My parents were vowing to challenge it still and all three parties faced off in court once again.

The truth was that I was almost 17 and the court would shortly have little or no jurisdiction over me. If I just left and went to my grandmother's, it would become a question of whether I was in a safe place or not. I had a family member with a stable home ready to take me in. It was a slam-dunk, and yet my parents were still fighting it.

The worst feeling was that I had earned my right to leave the group home. I had worked hard to follow the rules and do well in school. I had passed my sophomore year and was on track to finish my junior year on the high honor roll. I went from dropping out of school to missing only three days. I did all that was asked of me and more, and now my parents wanted me to stay in the group home or go to foster care? Could I do absolutely nothing right? That awful feeling was about to be overshadowed by an even worse one.

We were all in court discussing what was in my best interest. My parents continued to advocate that I stay where I was. We made the arguments that I had earned the right to leave and that I would continue to make progress at my grandmother's. As the court hearing continued it started to look like we would win.

Then the judge asked my parents a question the answer to which would stay with me for a long time. "What if I ordered him home?"

My father responded with a straight face, "We don't want him home."

My heart sank. The feeling that I had suspected was true for a long time was finally acknowledged. I started to cry.

The affirmation was the final piece needed. Going home would not happen even if I spent more time in a group home. I had done what was required and the judge agreed. I was going to live with my grandmother. It had been more than a year since I left home, and two years since I had first tried to commit suicide and ended up on probation in the first place. I had won, but I had lost so much. Then I was asked to sacrifice a little more. This time my grandmother and social worker were asking me to stay in the group home longer.

My only thought was "you have to be kidding me!" We just went through all of that to get me out, and now I was being asked to stay. Not for a year, but two months so that I could finish out the school year. The decision was mine and mine alone. I decided to stay. I had come to realize that the group home was a good thing for me. I had grown and become a better person. I was happier than I had ever been.

It was 14 months after I walked onto the campus, I walked away for good.

Life Goes On

I survived a few years of hell and came out the other side a better person. Shortly after moving into my grandmother's, I got my driver's license, a car, and a full-time job for the summer. I graduated from high school and trade school and not only became the electrician I wanted to be, but I ran my own company that I started while still in high school. I did a stint in the Navy and eventually found my way to college. I got married, and now I am a middle school teacher. I try to pass on the tough lessons I learned in an attempt to help someone avoid what I went through.

Life was tough for a while and my relationship with my parents didn't improve until many years later. I sincerely hope that this book does not create another rift between us. I hope that they understand my need to get this story out in the hopes it will help others. You never totally get over the emotions of events like the ones I went through, but I learned to surround myself with positive people, and they helped me tremendously when times got hard.

I have persevered. I have survived. Life goes on.

Epilogue

Writing this has been an interesting adventure. It began a decade ago as more of a way for me to work out the feelings I had. I would write some then put it down for long periods of time. After about three years, it started to take the form of a book. There were titles that looked like rough chapter headings and a bunch of words in between. I decided to turn it into a book, but never thought I would actually finish it nor did I think I would ever publish it.

I have written it in the hopes that it helps a family avoid the pitfalls that mine fell into. Maybe it will help someone who is going through something similar, or has already gone through it, to not feel as alone as I did. It took me years to even admit that I was in a group home and even longer to talk about the other events. It was a tragic time in my history, but it shaped me into who I am today and I don't honestly know if I would change it and do things differently.

That being said, I want to talk about perspective. One of the reasons it took seven years from the time I decided to turn my story into a book and the time it took to finish this relatively short publication was the perspective in which I was going to write it. I tried many times to write it as I see things now. As you age and have more life experiences, your view of things changes. As a teacher I say and do things I thought were totally unfair as a kid. I understand things better now, and I had a hard time writing my story in a way that made any sense at all. I chose to write from the perspective I had back then. This was not easy and brought back many feelings and events I had forgotten. This proved to be the natural format for my story.

Everything I have written is true, but my goal was never to make anyone look or feel bad. I left out details that served only to make a person out as a villain or a hero. I know that this will bring back painful memories, but I sincerely hope my family will understand why I had to put this information out there. It helps no one to keep this information to myself when I believe it really has the power to help someone.

There were no winners in this. We all lost a bit of ourselves. Families are a tricky thing, but I believe that you have to put bad times and hurt feelings behind you and just love each other.

I don't blame my parents for anything that happened to me, and I don't blame anyone else, including myself. Many things could have been done differently, but I sincerely feel that my parents were trying their best. To say I was a difficult child is an understatement. My parents did what they thought was right. Things just went too far. My family was destroyed in large part due to my actions. My sisters are survivors as well and I can never say I am sorry enough for the hell I put them through. I hope that have forgiven me.

Life can throw a lot at you and sometimes all you can do is duck. The scars of events more than a decade and a half ago are still healing. The hardest thing to do was acknowledge that they exist and work together to get past them.

I fell down hard and often, but I never stayed down for long. I had a lot of help and probably an equal amount of luck, but I worked hard and survived the falls.

Falling Down

A Teenager's True Story of
Redemption

Daniel P. Kelly

About the Author

Daniel Kelly is a middle school teacher who strives to help the students he sees following the same path he once went down.

He regularly volunteers for at-risk children's programs and gives talks to youth, parents, caregivers, and youth-care workers.

Kelly lives in Durham, NC with his wife and two dogs, Katie and Pharaoh.

Other Information

For book ordering, speaking, or any other information, please visit fallingdownbook.com or email info@fallingdownbook.com.

To find out how you can help children in need with a financial donation, please visit the website or email donate@fallingdownbook.com.

See the following pages for contact information for hotline numbers if you or someone you know is in crisis.

You can make a difference...

Toll-Free Crisis Hotline Numbers

Child Abuse

Childhelp®
Phone: 800.4.A.CHILD (800.422.4453)
People They Help: Child abuse victims,
parents, concerned individuals

Child Sexual Abuse

Darkness to Light
Phone: 866.FOR.LIGHT (866.367.5444)
People They Help: Children and adults
needing local information or resources
about sexual abuse

Family Violence

National Domestic Violence Hotline
Phone: 800.799.SAFE (800.799.7233)
TTY: 800.787.3224
Video Phone Only for Deaf Callers:
206.518.9361
People They Help: Children, parents,
friends, offenders

Help for Parents

National Parent Helpline®
Phone: 855.4APARENT (855.427.2736)
(Available 10 a.m. to 7 p.m., PST, weekdays)
People They Help: Parents and caregivers needing emotional support and links to resources

Human Trafficking

National Human Trafficking Hotline
Phone: 888.373.7888
People They Help: Victims of human trafficking and those reporting potential trafficking situations

Mental Illness

National Alliance on Mental Illness
Phone: 800.950.NAMI (800.950.6264)
(Available 10 a.m. to 6 p.m., ET, weekdays)
People They Help: Individuals, families, professionals

Missing/Abducted Children

Child Find of America
Phone: 800.I.AM.LOST (800.426.5678)
People They Help: Parents reporting lost
or abducted children, including parental
abductions

Child Find of America—Mediation
Phone: 800.A.WAY.OUT (800.292.9688)
People They Help: Parents (abduction,
prevention, child custody issues)

National Center for Missing and Exploited Children
Phone: 800.THE.LOST (800.843.5678)
TTY: 800.826.7653
People They Help: Families and
professionals (social services, law
enforcement)

Substance Abuse

National Alcohol and Substance Abuse Information Center
Phone: 800.784.6776

People They Help: Families,
professionals, media, policymakers,
concerned individuals

Suicide Prevention

National Suicide Prevention Lifeline
Phone: 800.273.TALK (800.273.8255)
TTY: 800.799.4TTY (800.799.4889)
People They Help: Families, concerned
individuals

Youth in Trouble/ Runaways

National Runaway Switchboard
Phone: 800.RUNAWAY (800.786.2929)
People They Help: Runaway and
homeless youth, families

Information obtained from:
Child Welfare Information Gateway.
(2012). Toll-free crisis hotline numbers.
Washington, DC: U.S. Department of
Health and Human Services, Children's
Bureau.

25995550R00080

Made in the USA
Charleston, SC
21 January 2014